Designing Ritual

Celebrating the Sacred
in the Ordinary

by Fr. James Telthorst

Richard White

Felicia Wolf, O.S.F.

Scripture excerpts taken from the *New American Bible* © 1991, 1986, 1970 Confraternity of Christian Doctrine, Washington, D.C.

Living the Good News
    a division of the Morehouse Group
Editorial Offices
600 Grant St., Suite 400
James R. Creasey, Publisher

Published in cooperation with Buena Vista, Inc.
P.O. Box 745475
Arvada, CO 80006
bv@buenavista.org
www.buenavista.org
303-477-0180

Originally published by Buena Vista Inc. as *Ritual: Celebrating the Sacred in th Ordinary*, 1997

ISBN 1-931960-08-9

CONTENTS

Foreword

Since 1987, Buena Vista has been networking
small Christian communities and offering support
and resources for forming and nurturing SCCs.

Buena Vista members believe that being Christian
and being church are synonymous. They also believe that church and community are synonymous.
Therefore, it follows that being a Christian means
being in community. Or, stated another way, living
the Christian life outside of community is impos-
sible. For most of us, the experience of church
is within the parish or congregation, mainly in
a large group on Sunday morning. The recent
reemergence of small communities—within
parishes and through religious congregations—
has brought renewal, hope and a way to break
down the large size of most congregations making community and church more relevant.

The Christian church at its roots is about small
groups gathering in homes to remember Jesus
and to be sent into the world to proclaim the love
of God. These activities from our deepest tradition
are what it means to be church. The booklets in
this series are designed to help groups focus on
becoming church.

As a grassroots, Catholic organization, Buena Vista
has taken a biblical version of church and applied
it to the life of small communities. The vision con-
sists of four dimensions: *koinonoia*—mutuality,
love and care within the community; *diakonia*—
service and striving for justice within and outside
of the community; *leitourgia*—praying and sacra-
mentalizing the life of the community; and

kerygma—being grounded in the Christian story. Our mission statement affirms four fundamental essentials of church and of SCCs: mutuality/community, service/justice, prayer/ritual and scripture/gospel-based witness. With this printing of the small community resource booklets, Buena Vista updates the first four volumes in our series designed to create conversation within and among SCCs.

Through these resources for small communities, we offer an opportunity for new and experienced groups to focus on essential activities of small Christian community life. Each booklet may be used independently or in succession with the other volumes. Each was written by a team of experienced small community practitioners who draw on their connection with the Buena Vista network of small Christian communities and years of ministry in facilitation and training for small Christian community development.

Creating Community helps your SCC to look at what shapes its identity and interior life as a small community, and provides background about the need for community as we become church. *Living Scripture* weaves the universal story of salvation into the small group experience, focusing on the deep meaning it gives to our lives as individuals and as a community. It explores our relationship as individuals and communities to the Great Stories of God's salvation, providing guidance for reflection on scripture and its use in small Christian communities. *Designing Ritual* helps small communities to understand the role of ritual prayer in expressing the sacredness of life. It contains practical steps for designing rituals for use in your own small Christian community. *Seeking Justice* addresses the public life of faith—why and how our SCCs are called to respond to scripture by making a difference in the greater community—with steps for community discernment and models for action.

The booklets in the series can be used in any order. They are appropriate for deepening the experience of small communities that have been meeting for years, or as an introduction to small Christian community for new groups.

With gratitude to the original authors, former Buena Vista national coordinator Barb Darling, recent reviewers, and our editors at Living the Good News, we offer these updated volumes for use by your small Christian communities. Each booklet contains useful information about the topic it addresses in the context of six easy-to-use small community sessions. We hope the dialogue within and among groups will be fruitful and challenging, leading to more effective mission. We look forward to hearing your reflections about the essentials of community on which your group chooses to focus, and about their reality in the experience of your SCC, and in the network of SCCs that our membership comprises. Enjoy one another as you deepen your faith and engage in discovery about your relationship with God in community.

Amy Sheber Howard
Buena Vista Executive Director
National Coordinator

Introduction

This booklet will help individuals and communities understand the human desire for ritual as well as help them feel comfortable in designing ritual and in praying together. As the sessions explain the distinctiveness of Catholic ritual, they help the reader to understand that ritual expresses the sacredness of life. Getting beyond a perfunctory recitation of the Lord's Prayer, communities can learn to incorporate symbols and song, scripture and the events of ordinary life into meaningful experiences of prayer. Using the practical examples and thoughtful questions, small communities will undoubtedly develop a deeper and richer life of prayer and ritual.

Which number do you think is larger, the number of Catholics that Bishops report as part of the United States population or the number of people that report themselves as Catholics to the Gallup poll? You probably guessed correctly that the numbers who report themselves as Catholic are much larger than the Bishops' official numbers.

Those often referred to as "alienated" Catholics feel anything but. What keeps them feeling connected to our Church?

The answer is easy to see any Christmas or Easter or at any funeral or wedding. We may not understand it or be able to explain it, but many feel ritual is one of the strongest attractions of our Church. Even ministers of other denominations envy it. As one minister expressed it, "You Catholics have something in your ritual. For example, at a funeral, you don't just talk, you *do something* in your prayer."

The prayers and rituals that are such an important element of small Christian communities are both similar to and different from the prayers and rituals we've always performed in the larger assemblies of our parishes and the ones we perform individually. In small communities we are not attempting to create a separate and sacred space. As we gather in our homes and parish meeting halls, we dwell in a space where we recognize the sacred already present.

It is appropriate that individuals plan a communal ritual prayer. It is definitely a requirement that the entire community engages in the communal ritual. It is too easy to allow our communal prayer to be reduced to a collection of prayers of individuals gathered with little appreciation of our communal identity.

These sessions serve as a community exercise in learning and sharing about what community ritual prayer is and what it can be. The goals of this booklet are to celebrate the rituals in which communities are already engaged and to encourage SCCs to enlarge their understanding and practice of ritual for their communal prayer/ritual life.

The primary intent for this booklet is use by small Christian communities and other small groups such as ministry committees. However, it is appropriate as a learning tool for individuals as well. Group facilitators should plan for plenty of interaction time as you apply the principles to your own circumstances. In general, you will use one chapter or session for each meeting time. However, some small communities or groups may choose to spend several weeks on Sessions 5 and 6 if they would like extended time for members to practice designing the various types of ritual and using them in the community setting.

As you read this book alone or apply its principles together as a community, remember this paradox. Ritual is what we do because words and intellect are inadequate for what only ritual provides; yet, we use words and intellect here to understand and appreciate ritual!

Thank you to a small group of people from St. Patrick's Catholic Community in Scottsdale, Arizona who helped create some of the session elements in the revised edition of this volume.

Session One
RITUAL IN YOUR COMMUNITY

Scripture

Facilitator asks someone who has prepared ahead to read the scripture aloud:

> They devoted themselves to the teaching of the apostles and to the communal life, to the breaking of the bread and to the prayers. Awe came upon everyone, and many wonders and signs were done through the apostles. All who believed were together and had all things in common; they would sell their property and possessions and divide them among all according to each one's need. Every day they devoted themselves to meeting together in the temple area and to breaking bread in their homes. They ate their meals with exultation and sincerity of heart, praising God and enjoying favor with all the people. And every day the Lord added to their number those who were being saved.
>
> —*Acts 2:42-47*

Focus Question

In groups of two, take five minutes to prepare for the gathering by discussing:

○ What rituals did the apostles experience with each other in the early Christian communities?

Sharing Questions

Discuss:

O How would a news reporter who came to visit your community report your gathering so that all would know you were a small Christian community (SCC) instead of a discussion group?

O Your responses to the following questions will help you answer the question above. Share insights in groups of 3 or 4 for about 30 minutes.

— What happens as members walk in the door for a meeting? As members leave?

— Are there other patterns for what you do at each meeting time: Who talks when? Making decisions?

— What role does silence play?

— How do you acknowledge the needs of group members?

— How do you acknowledge life events such as graduations, birthdays, anniversaries, etc.?

— How do you expand your consciousness of and address the world's realities?

In answering these questions, you have answered how your group is already using ritual.

Commentary

Facilitator reads this passage aloud, or invites a volunteer to read it:

Rituals are at the core of the social identity of all small communities. Rituals are repeated actions that hold meaning, bring comfort and lead to creativity. Rituals are a way to be attentive to the sacred in the movements and moments of community life so that they are not lost or not

11

reflected upon. They solemnize and raise from the context of the ordinary to an articulated level those things that would otherwise pass unnoticed in the life of the community or its individual members. Rituals reconcile us with the way things are, even when the way things are may be chaotic or tragic.

Development of a ritual attitude is important in the life of a community. It involves being attentive to the way the community recognizes and acknowledges God's presence and activity in the life of that community.

Shared Prayer

Facilitator invites group members to quiet themselves for prayer, then reads this prayer aloud:

> Loving God, we hold in prayer before you all the concerns of our hearts and our lives. As a community we now share our prayers of thankfulness and of petition.

At this time, members share intentions for the community and personal intentions.

Closing Prayer

Gracious God, please help us to see you in all we experience in the coming weeks. Help us to identify more clearly your presence in our daily rituals and in the rituals of this SCC. Be with us as we explore ways to become closer and experience your presence in all we do. *Amen.*

Session Two

ADAPT, ADAPT, ADAPT!

Scripture

Facilitator asks someone who has prepared ahead
to read the scripture aloud:

> What was from the beginning, what we have
> heard, what we have seen with our eyes, what
> we looked upon and touched with our hands
> concerns the Word of life—for the life was
> made visible; we have seen it and testify to it
> and proclaim to you the eternal life that was
> with the Father and was made visible to us—
> what we have seen and heard we proclaim now
> to you, so that you too may have fellowship
> with us; for our fellowship is with the Father
> and with his Son, Jesus Christ. We are writing
> this so that our joy may be complete.
>
> —*1 John 1:1-4*

Focus

Share in pairs for about 20 minutes:

○ Imagine yourself sitting in your favorite easy
  chair reflecting on this scripture passage. Aloud
  or in writing, express what you would say.
○ Imagine yourself sitting at a kitchen table with
  a couple of friends. Aloud or in writing, tell your
  friends what you think of the scriptural quote.
○ Now imagine yourself leading a catechumenate
  gathering. Aloud or in writing, tell the group
  what you think of the scriptural quote.

13

Commentary I:
Differences in Ritual

Facilitator leads the discussion saying:

The previous focus experience enables us to consider the difference between private (individual)
devotion, small community ritual and public (large
assembly) ritual. Some of the differences might be:
○ preparation time
○ formality/informality
○ physical space and surroundings
○ whether or not the speakers are apt to be
  looked upon as expert
○ amount of scrutiny the presentation is given
  by those experiencing or observing it

Facilitator then invites the group:
○ Tell about some other differences that you have
  experienced.

Adapting anything, whether from private devotion
to small Christian community ritual or from public
ritual to small Christian community ritual, requires
change to make it effective. Some people in the
early stages of designing ritual and prayer may
want to use outside resources, including some of
those mentioned in the Further Reading section
at the end of this booklet.

Commentary II: Adapting Public
Ritual to Small Communities

Facilitator reads aloud:

During the Easter Vigil at our parishes the people
are blessed with holy water sprinkled over them.
In small community gatherings in homes, the

water could be passed among the group and sipped or the water could be used to mark the sign of the cross on each person's forehead or palm. Both are signs of blessing.

Sharing Questions

Discuss:

○ Name another familiar, public, ritual action that your SCC has performed after adapting it to your group.

— How did you begin the ritual differently than in the large assembly?

— How did you pray differently than in the large assembly?

— What cultural differences and physical realities came into play?

— What did you experience as successful and why?

Commentary III: Adapting Private Devotions to Small Communities

Facilitator reads this passage aloud:

The Stations of the Cross developed in Jerusalem. They evolved into a private devotion where a person could walk in the steps of Jesus, therefore entering more deeply into the memory of Jesus' passion. In an attempt to adapt this prayer to our large parish assemblies, the walking was relegated to a single person or several persons only. The rest of the community watched. Remembering group stations, if you are old enough, helps you understand a traditionally individual prayer form used as a communal prayer form.

Sharing Questions

Discuss:

○ How would you adapt the Stations of the Cross to a meaningful small community ritual?

○ What other traditionally private devotions have you adapted or could you adapt for your community's use?

○ Which adaptations have you experienced as successful and why?

Action

Facilitator invites a volunteer to read this passage aloud:

Most published resources for prayer and ritual are just the starting point for your preparation and must be considered generic. They need a soul to put your community in touch with God. You can be the one to adapt those bare bones prayers and rituals to the soul of the community with whom you will be praying. Take a look at the resources you use in your community and see how you would add ritual or ritualize those "bare bones." Bring your ideas to our next meeting.

Shared Prayer

Facilitator invites group members to quiet themselves for prayer, then reads this prayer aloud:

Loving God, we hold in prayer before you all the concerns of our hearts and our lives. As a community we now share our prayers of thankfulness and of petition.

At this time, members share intentions for the community and personal intentions.

Closing Prayer

Decide as a group how you would like to close your meeting to make the experience meaningful to each of you.

Session Three
WHAT MAKES A RITUAL "CATHOLIC"?

Scripture

Facilitator asks someone who has prepared ahead
to read the scripture aloud:

> Before the feast of Passover, Jesus knew that his
> hour had come to pass from this world to the
> Father. He loved his own in the world and he
> loved them to the end. The devil had already in-
> duced Judas, son of Simon the Iscariot, to hand
> him over. So, during supper, fully aware that the
> Father had put everything into his power and
> that he had come from God and was returning
> to God, he rose from supper and took off his
> outer garments. He took a towel and tied it
> around his waist. Then he poured water into a
> basin and began to wash the disciples' feet and
> dry them with the towel around his waist. He
> came to Simon Peter, who said to him, "Master,
> are you going to wash my feet?" Jesus answered
> and said to him, "What I am doing, you do not
> understand now, but you will understand later."
> Peter said to him, "You will never wash my feet."
> Jesus answered him, "Unless I wash you, you
> will have no inheritance with me." Simon Peter
> said to him, "Master, then not only my feet, but
> my hands and head as well."
>
> —*John 13:1-9*

Focus Question

Share in pairs for about 20 minutes:

○ Imagine you are the movie director, Martin Scorsese. For your next film you are designing a scene to look Catholic. What would you place in the scene to create a Catholic atmosphere?

○ You also want to quickly establish a character as Catholic. What would you have the character do to show he/she is a Catholic?

In answering these questions, you have discussed two important elements of Catholic ritual: *sacred objects* and *sacred actions.*

Commentary I: Elements of a Catholic Ritual

Take turns reading the following commentary aloud, with a new reader for each section:

There are six important elements of ritual. They do not all have to be used every time or in the same pattern. Look at them as if they were the primary colors of red, blue and yellow. You are an artist. You can mix them to produce other colors that your community likes.

Symbols

We take our sacred symbols from the ordinary. We use ordinary water, ordinary bread, ordinary wine, ordinary olive oil and ordinary gestures for our most public rituals. But when designing or adapting ritual for a small Christian community or another small group, one must already possess a certain contemplative view of water, oil, earth, fire or meal to appreciate the revelatory character within the ritual.

These symbols are, by definition, messy. They are not always neat and, while organized in the ritual, still need to reflect that natural earthy messiness: bread does crumble, water is wet and sometimes cold and oil runs. Candles, lamps, incense, light and darkness should also be considered when choosing symbols which reveal the sacredness of the ordinary.

Scripture

The Bible contains our most sacred stories. That is why they are used frequently in our rituals. When you read scripture in a small group setting, always have this question before you, "Why, of all the stories about God, does our faith tradition need to remember this one?"

Each of the stories are answers to the basic human questions that our ancestors asked, although the answers may not be rational or logical. Catholics use the Bible as a prayer book, as a springboard for meditation, as a source of wisdom. Our goal is not to memorize the Bible (although we may), but to enter into the stories and move around in them. We do this so that we become the story.

Music

Music may be neglected, but is needed in SCC rituals. One reason for its neglect is that many of us mistake the performance of music with music as prayer. Singing together is one of the most intimate acts a group can perform. To sing, a group has to breathe together, feel the same rhythm together and say the same words together. All at the same time! We are connected at our very centers.

A group that feels it can't sing together or without skilled musicians or recorded music should try this experiment. Someone begin singing "Happy Birthday" or "Take Me Out to the Ball Game." Take note of and discuss what happened.

Singing isn't the only way to use music in ritual. Use of recorded background music for reflection time, use of a bell or the rhythmic easy back and forth of a saying a psalm or a litany alternately can also be musical.

Actions
Actions begin with reverence. A simple touch, a sensitive and welcoming look, our prayer posture, open or closed eyes, making the sign of the cross —each of these can be so commonplace as to be mediocre. Or the gesture can be used to animate and raise the commonplace to the sacramental. Can we stand for prayer or do we always sit? Are there occasions when we would kneel? Many people join hands but we shouldn't be restricted to one gesture. Human embraces are expressed in many ways (sometimes awkwardly), but it is certainly appropriate to bless one another in some way, perhaps signing each with the cross as we send them forth, accompanying each other into the world of our work and mission.

Silence
Einstein said he could prove the relativity of time by asking, "What is the difference in the experience of one minute sitting on a hot radiator and

another minute sitting next to a pretty girl?"The statement may be politically incorrect, but the point is well taken. Words may be barriers to communication. There need to be breathing spaces in every ritual to let the Holy Spirit enter and do the work that the planner of the ritual could not do.

In this age of noise—TV, radio, CDs, traffic and computers—we are often nervous with silence. How long should we be silent? Several short interludes of silence are probably more effective than one long session. Remember the example of Einstein and simply watch for audible sighs or fidgeting, a sure way to tell that the radiator has gotten hot!

Life
Sacramental people who raise up the holiness of the ordinary bring the events of our lives to ritual. Our liturgical calendar uses the structure of the seasons annually. We celebrate birth, grief, joy, marriage, events in the news, death, anger. Everything is holy; everything can be brought to prayer and ritual. If we bring only what we judge to be polite or churchworthy, we will limit our experience of the power and depth of ritual.

Sharing Question
○ What does this Commentary say to you? What would you add?
○ To what extent is your community incorporating these elements?

Commentary II:
The Liturgical Year

Small Christian communities easily use the lectionary to study scripture and share faith, but using the liturgical year as a basis for prayer and ritual is more obscure. Our church uses the liturgical year to focus its design of rituals for the larger assembly. Employing the same strategy in community rituals will keep the SCC connected with the larger church.

Here are some ideas for focus and elements to use when planning rituals based in the Catholic liturgical seasons:

Advent
○ songs of expectation
○ Advent wreath
○ Feast of the Immaculate Conception
○ Feast of Our Lady of Guadalupe
○ anniversary of the deaths of Ita Ford, Dorothy Kazel, Jeanne Donovan, Maura Clark
○ St. Nicholas Day

Christmas
○ tree decorating
○ Jesse Tree
○ Epiphany

Ordinary Time after Christmas
○ St. Blaise Day
○ St. Patrick's Day

Lent
○ almsgiving
○ fasting

Triduum
○ foot-washing
○ veneration of the cross

Eastertime
○ white decorations
○ new life
○ lilies

Ordinary Time after Easter
○ stories of the early church
○ gardens and flowers

Fall
○ celebrating harvest
○ honoring of migrant workers/celebrating the birthday of Cesar Chavez
○ All Saints
○ St. Francis of Assisi

Sharing Question

Discuss:
○ In light of the liturgical year:
  — Which sacred symbol speaks most clearly to you and why?
  — What environment helps you feel "holy"?
  — Which liturgical season is your favorite?
  — When in your life has a touch, sound or smell had a profound meaning or recalled a profound moment?

Action

Before your next community meeting, think of additional suggestions you could add to the above list of rituals throughout the liturgical year that would be meaningful for your own group's ritual practice. Share these with the group at the beginning of your next session.

Shared Prayer

Facilitator invites group members to quiet themselves for prayer, then reads this prayer aloud:

> Loving God, we hold in prayer before you all the concerns of our hearts and our lives. As a community we now share our prayers of thankfulness and of petition.

At this time, members share intentions for the community and personal intentions.

Closing Prayer

Good and gracious God, we thank you for this time of sharing and we ask your blessings on each of us as we go out this week to bring about the reign of God in our families and environments. We now give each other a blessing by placing the sign of the cross on each person's forehead and offering a sign of peace. *Amen.*

Session Four
ANXIETIES AND CAUTIONS

Scripture
In a moment of quiet, think of the various scripture stories you know. Reflect on which scripture story resonates most strongly with you at this moment. You do not have to know the entire story, simply what is speaking to you right now.

Focus
Share in pairs for about 10 minutes your reflection on what scripture story resonates with you most strongly at this moment.

Commentary
Four people take turns reading aloud the introduction and the three sections that follow:

Introduction
Because Catholics have traditionally relied on the institution for initiating prayer and ritual and on ordained leaders of prayer and ritual, lay people may feel insecure about initiating or adapting rituals for small Christian communities.

When planning ritual and prayer for our community, we need to keep in mind that prayers and blessings don't happen because a priest (or anyone else) "says" them or "does" them. Nor does prayer "make" God "do something." A religious ritual doesn't manipulate God to act lovingly toward us; it represents that love in visible, tangible form. It makes God's love real so that our minds can easily grasp it and our hearts and spirits can be infused with it.

Theology of Ritual

Ritualistic prayers are not merely expressions of ideas or concepts. Theology certainly attempts to explain realities and mysteries, but placing theology first too easily reduces the elements to the minimal, to an ordered and sometimes sterile presence. Herein lies a modern and ongoing error. Creating our own rituals, we too easily begin with an idea or concept, then tell the assembly what the action is supposed to mean. In doing so, we presume that intellect and understanding are primary and the most important ingredient. Ritual elements are basic human acts which, when done with reverence, reveal a presence otherwise ignored, forgotten or seldom encountered.

Ritual is an experience that might need some intelligent reflection later. But the experience must not depend solely on logic for its design, and finding a central theme is often a contrivance. Rather than a theme, the real need in ritual design is a focus.

Ritual Takes Time

Ritual cannot be created overnight but develops over time. Ritual forms us as people by repetition. Yet, when celebrated well, it is not simply routine. It's important to remember that, once you have found the right mix of colors that we talked about in the beginning of this session, changing that mix too often or on a whim can be detrimental to an otherwise good ritual. Ritual, by its nature, does have a certain pattern or routine, thus freeing us to think and be concerned not so much about the order but about the greater reality of the pattern.

Rather than creating or manipulating feelings, ritual ultimately changes attitudes, the ways we see, think, perceive, respond to life and to the world. In other words, it is ultimately about conversion which is probably, over time, why ritual works on us like water on a rock.

Borrowing from Other Cultures

Small Christian communities may feel it is difficult to create a new ritual without "borrowing" from another culture. We often feel we need to turn to either New Age or ancient native American cultures, for instance, to do something ritualistic. Then we become apprehensive about being "too creative." How do we know when we're straying too far into cultic or New Age ritual and away from common Catholic, Christian practices? Sometimes it's difficult to walk that line between superstition and faithful prayer.

A cult is a small group that practices rituals which are valued because they are secret. The rituals maintain power because so few can perform them. The struggle of our Church to change our ritual language from Latin to the language of the people was a rejection of the cultic. Latin became our ritual language when it was the most widely used language in the world. But when Latin was no longer common, it became a secret language that few understood. So the language of our ritual changed to the languages that people could understand.

A cult performs a ritual so that the members can have an influence on God. Catholics perform a ritual so that the participants become more open to God's influence on them. Cults boast that they and no one else have God's favor. Catholic theology clearly says that our church is not the reign of God. Our church takes on the mission of making the world the reign of God. We perform our rituals so that we can be open to God's influence in this great mission.

Sharing Questions

With a partner, discuss:

○ Describe a ritual you've experienced as contrived and sterile. Why were you not able to fully enter into this ritual?

○ Think back to the description above of ritual affecting us "like water on a rock." Name a ritual act that you do with your family or your small community that has taken on deeper meaning as time has gone by.

○ From your experience and study, what are some other differences between cultic, New Age and Catholic small Christian community ritual?

Action

Reflect this week on what rituals you are most hesitant about, especially when it comes to using them in your families. Attempt to identify those and ask yourself why you are uncomfortable and what can you do to experience them anyway.

Shared Prayer

Facilitator invites group members to quiet themselves for prayer, then reads this prayer aloud:

> Loving God, we hold in prayer before you all
> the concerns of our hearts and our lives. As a
> community we now share our prayers of thank-
> fulness and of petition.

At this time, members share intentions for the
community and personal intentions.

Closing Prayer

Gather together in a circle, facing out, holding
hands, and say an "Our Father" as a sign of your
willingness to take the Word into the world.

Session Five
DESIGNING A RITUAL

Scripture

Facilitator asks someone who has prepared ahead to read the scripture aloud:

> There are different kinds of spiritual gifts but the same Spirit; there are different forms of service but the same Lord; there are different workings but the same God who produces all of them in everyone. To each individual the manifestation of the Spirit is given for some benefit. To one is given through the Spirit the expression of wisdom; to another the expression of knowledge according to the same Spirit; to another faith by the same Spirit; to another gifts of healing by the one Spirit; to another mighty deeds; to another prophecy; to another discernment of spirits; to another varieties of tongues; to another interpretation of tongues. But one and the same Spirit produces all of these, distributing them individually to each person as he wishes.
>
> *—1 Corinthians 12:4-11*

Focus

Gather in groups of three or four for about 20 minutes and share:

- During the past few meetings, what have you learned about the gifts you have to offer your community?
- What gifts do you see in the members of your community that will help with ritual?

31

Commentary

Take turns in the group reading the following considerations for planning ritual.

While large and small groups experience ritual in community, planning ritual is not always a group effort. It may work for your small Christian community to have two or three members responsible for planning prayer. However, a ritual needs focus, and it's difficult for more than one person to organize the planning and the calling together. For this reason, we now change the emphasis in our text to the singular planner rather than the communal experience. Anyone who plans should consider four steps.

Four Steps to Success
Step One: Focus and Considerations

Determine what things you should consider about the group you are planning for and think about the needs that will be brought to ritual. Keep these needs and considerations in your own prayer during the planning period, for example:

○ Who is the group? Are they teenagers or the middle-aged? Immigrants, students or church staff? An ecumenical mixture?

○ What is the time of day? Morning when all are perky and the sun is shining through the windows? Evening after a full day of work in a room with florescent lighting?

○ How much time is set aside for this ritual? A short period before a longer discussion of momentous issues? Before a social time? Is this a gathering specifically to experience prayer and ritual?

○ Where will the prayer take place? In a church basement or a recreation room complete with ping-pong table? Out of doors on the grass or in a comfy living room with soft chairs?

Step Two: Elements of Catholic Ritual
Consider:

○ What elements can you sensibly incorporate into the prayer? How do you set a visual and tangible tone?

○ What symbols are readily available? A bright tablecloth draped on a coffee table? The elements of oil, water or candles? An item of specific significance to the group?

○ How will scripture enter into your ritual? The family Bible? Who will read scripture, and which passage?

○ How will you use music? Are you willing to introduce song into the group a capella? Will you use recorded music as accompaniment or as background?

○ What actions will we use? Reverencing the Bible or blessing with holy water? How can silence play a meaningful part?

○ What event is the central focus of this ritual? World and community events? Lectionary-based scripture? Conflict in our own community?

Step Three: Outline of the Ritual
Like most symphonies, most rituals have three movements; it helps to base your outline on these movements:

○ *Gathering:* When individuals gather into a communal whole, something happens; a collective
person is formed. This person is unlike any individual in the group yet it is like all the individuals in the group. When we gather we need to
use time and gentleness so that this collective
person can come to life.

○ *Event:* When this collective person comes to
life, the question is, "Why?" What does this person do? Who is this person?

○ *Conclusion:* When the community separates, it
is the dissolution of a communal person. If we
are not attentive to the leaving process, there
will be a sense of incompleteness in the individual members.

Step Four: Walk-Through

After you've written down an outline of your ritual, you may have the luxury of asking the group
to respond to what you have designed and to give
their input. If not, walk through your design in
your mind. Adjust what doesn't make sense.

Now, as the commercial says, "Just do it!"
Remember there are no mistakes in prayer,
only improvements in design.

Examples For Practice

Facilitator asks two people ahead of time to read
each of the following two examples to the group.
Community members should follow along and
note what sounds workable and what could
change.

Example #1

Step One: Focus and Considerations

I am meeting with my SCC group: mostly middle-aged adults, active in the same parish. We are, by and large, professionals with a college education: mostly women and several men. In general, the women in our group love environment and details and the men love big concepts and ideas. Recently we have been studying the book *Soulmates* by Thomas Moore.

We meet in each other's homes from 7:30-9:30 on Friday evenings. Even though people are tired they generally are not worried about how late the meeting goes because the next day is Saturday. This week we will gather in Jane's living room with low, easy chairs. I need to remember it's hard to get out of these chairs once we get into them.

We had an intense meeting last time. The book we were discussing is about relationships. Many in the group were reminded of some painful relationship in their past. We need to forgive ourselves for what we think are failures. It is Lent and our parish is using the theme of "going into the desert."

Step Two: Elements

A great visual would be for each person to use their fingers or a stick to write in a large box of sand the name of the person with whom they had a painful relationship. But, then I remember we need a movement that can be done without getting out of low, soft chairs. I think that maybe we can pass a small container of sand around instead.

The song I always sing in Lent is, "Shepherd me,
O God, beyond my wants, beyond my fears, from
death into life." I think it fits with broken relationships and I feel comfortable initiating the singing.

Step Three: Outline

○ *Gathering:* We will gather in the living room
which contains a large coffee table. I have
draped a purple cloth on the table and place
on it one saucer of sand. I will ask everyone to
sit quietly in their seats, breathing gently while
waiting for their spirits to catch up with where
their bodies have gathered.

○ *Event:* We will sing together "Shepherd Me,
O God." I will ask the group to pass the sand
around and ask what difficult relationship
comes to mind as they hold the sand. After each
person who wishes to names that relationship,
we will bless them by singing the refrain again.
Those who do not wish to name the relationship aloud may say "pass" and we will sing the
refrain as a blessing on their relationship in the
same way. We will continue our meeting with
our discussion of *Soulmates* and what it means
to our everyday lives.

○ *Conclusion:* At the end of the meeting we will
all take some sand into our hands and sing the
song again. Then we will adjourn to our coffee
and snacks.

Step Four: Walk-Through

After I "walked through" this ritual in my mind,
I could not figure out what I would do with the
sand in my hand after the last song. The possibility
of letting it fall into Jane's carpet seems to ruin

the mood—and my friendship with Jane. Perhaps putting the sand back into the saucer placed on the floor or a coffee table in the middle of our group after the song could be part of the ritual. Or I could gather some small plastic bags for us to put the sand in and take home to aid our Lenten reflection.

I wonder, "Is the saucer big enough for all this action?" I decide it is not and plan to use the large flowerpot dish on my porch instead. Also, just ending the first section with no transition to the discussion feels wrong. I will read Psalm 23 to conclude that section.

Example #2
Step One: Focus and Considerations
I am in charge of scheduling lectors in my parish. Several of us have started a scripture reflection group. This meets our small group needs and prepares us for our ministry of reading. Because I schedule, I am considered the leader. We did not meet formally during July and August. This will be our first meeting for a while. It also feels like the beginning of a new year. Our reflection time is powerful prayer.

We meet in the rectory basement in a room a little larger than we need each Monday from 7–8 PM. Our group is high energy, and the hard, straight-backed chairs make it easy to suggest movement. We all tend to be agitated lately because the pastor decided to change the church decorations without consulting any parishioners. It also seems appropriate to initiate a ritual for our Ministry of the Word in the beginning of the ministry year.

Step Two: Elements

I choose to use a candle I brought from home and the parish lectionary book. Because I would like to establish a prayerful environment before anyone can start talking about our conflict, I will ask the group to gather in silence.

Step Three: Outline

○ *Gathering:* Fifteen minutes before the gathering I will set a table in the middle of the room with the parish lectionary open on it and an unlit candle. I will also have some Gregorian chant music playing on the tape player I know is in the room. I will greet people and ask them to spend a few minutes in relaxing silence.

○ *Event:* When the group is gathered I will go to the candle, light it and welcome them back to another year by saying: "Where there are two or three gathered in the name of Jesus, there is Jesus. We are being Jesus for each other tonight."

— Approaching one of our members with the lectionary in my hand I will say the person's name and say, "This is the book of our sacred stories. Use it to proclaim truth." I bow as I give the book to that person and invite her to go to another person and do the same, using her own words if she chooses.

— When everyone has had a turn, we will read the week's scriptures out loud together and I will ask an opening question, such as "How did you experience another as Jesus tonight?" or "Did you feel you represented Jesus to another tonight?" or "How did this

week's readings speak to you tonight?" to
lead us into reflection.

○ *Conclusion:* At the end of our meeting we will
all join in singing a blessing for each other as
we begin this new year.

Step Four: Walk-Through

After walking through this ritual in my mind I real-
ize that I'm avoiding the conflict that is going on
in our parish. Conversation will inevitably turn to
that conflict later in the evening. I add a litany of
healing I found in a book to help us keep things
in perspective. I will ask people to spontaneously
offer petitions for healing for ourselves, our parish
and our world. If no one offers a petition for our
pastor and parishioners, I will have one ready.

Sharing Questions

Share in small groups your response to the
Commentary and to the Examples for Practice.
Tell each other what speaks to you and how you
think you can use this format in leading your SCC.
Name the kinds of ritual you'd like to lead, and
what elements you are uncomfortable with.

Action

It's Your Turn

Each person in the community should fill in the
worksheet below before your next session, using
additional paper as necessary. Use it to plan a
ritual for your community in the coming weeks.
Members may also choose to work in pairs to plan
a ritual.

Ritual Planning Worksheet

Name the community you will lead in ritual.

_____

Step One: Focus and considerations of the community

_____

_____

_____

Step Two: Elements
What elements makes sense for this ritual and which ones do you have easy access to, are you comfortable using, or do you want to stretch yourself to try?

_____

_____

_____

Step Three: Outline

Gathering	Event	Conclusion
_____	_____	_____
_____	_____	_____
_____	_____	_____
_____	_____	_____
_____	_____	_____
_____	_____	_____

Step Four: Walk Through
What feels awkward? What needs to be adjusted? If possible ask one or two members of your community to review your ritual and give you constructive suggestions.

_____

_____

_____

_____

Prayer

Facilitator invites group members to quiet themselves for prayer, then reads this prayer aloud:

> Loving God, we hold in prayer before you all
> the concerns of our hearts and our lives. As a
> community we now share our prayers of thank-
> fulness and of petition.

At this time, members share intentions for the
community and personal intentions.

Closing Prayer

In your own way, as a community, ask God to
guide you in the coming weeks as you plan a
ritual for your community.

At the end of the meeting, before breaking for
social time, get out a calendar and schedule dates
for each member to have an opportunity to lead
the group in ritual. You could do one ritual each
of the next several times your community gathers.
Or you could devote several sessions to practicing
ritual and experience the ritual designed by two
or three different community members in one
session. Reflect on the rituals at the end of each
of these sessions, until all members have had an
opportunity to lead the group in a ritual.

Session Six
ASSESSING A RITUAL

Your small community may choose to do this
session as a concluding session to your time spent
developing a deeper understanding of ritual. It
might be appropriate to use this session after several sessions of experiencing the rituals designed
by community members.

You may also choose to do Part II in the Sharing
section of this session after each of the rituals
your members lead, then go back and do the
whole session at the conclusion of the series
of sessions in which you experience the rituals
designed by each person.

Or your community may use this session immediately after Session Five, then begin the process of
experiencing the rituals designed by each member
over a series of group meetings.

*(The evaluation questions in Part II of the
Sharing section may be used as a reference in
the future to evaluate rituals used by the group
collectively or by individual group members in
other settings.)*

Scripture
Facilitator asks someone who has prepared ahead
to read the scripture aloud:

> In contrast, the fruit of the Spirit is love, joy,
> peace, patience, kindness, generosity, faithfulness,

gentleness, self-control. Against such there is no
law.

—Galatians 5:22-23

Focus

Break into groups of two and share with each
other for about 10 minutes. Discuss:
- ○ What speaks to you in this reading?
- ○ What fruits of the Spirit have you received/ex-
  perienced in your life?
- ○ How have you seen yourself or others in your
  community live out these fruits of the Spirit?

Commentary

Facilitator reads this passage aloud, or invites a
volunteer to read it:

Because a ritual is a combination of rational and
imaginative elements, it is an artful work that does
not fit categories well and cannot be evaluated
with a strict categorical measure. Assess it by
being attentive to signs within the group as well
as within yourself as the group convener.

Ritual is judged not so much as an Olympic event
with a numbering system, but as a meal is judged
by the mood of the group, the amount of food
that is eaten, the ease of conversation, etc.

Sharing Questions

Part I

Break into groups of 3 or 4 and share a story
about a ritual that spoke to you in a powerful way.

43

You may choose to ask members to take a few minutes to write the story first before sharing it in the small group.

Answer these questions:
○ What was the effect of that ritual on you?
○ What did you learn about yourself?

Part II
Share in the large group your experience of the rituals just discussed in the smaller group. Include the following elements:

Signs of Shifting Perspective
○ Immediately after a ritual and also later, do the people speak of seeing something more clearly, differently or with greater understanding?
○ Is there less talk about task oriented issues and more discussion about spiritual issues after the ritual?
○ Were you surprised by anything shared during the ritual?

Signs of Being Anchored in God
○ Is movement in the group slowing down?
○ Is the group more comfortable with faith sharing after the ritual?
○ Do people breathe in a relaxed manner before they do anything?
○ After the ritual is ended, does it take some time for the group to "come back"?

Signs of the Spirit
○ Was there a point in the ritual when you had a palpable sense that you were holding the group

while *you* were being held by a greater force?
○ Was a variety of emotions and thoughts shared?
○ Were there moments when you did not know
  what was going on yet felt safe?

Part III
Do an evaluation with your community about the
use of this Ritual Book. How has it been helpful to
your community? What did you learn?

Action

Final Commendations
If you are trying to enrich the rituals of your group
and you have worked through this guide, you are
a motivated group or individual and probably have
a good sense for ritual.

If you are never satisfied that you are good at designing ritual, you have a feel for the complexity
of the matter.

If you are afraid of being irreverent yet enjoy trying new things, you will never be irreverent.

If you sometimes feel awkward and foolish when
you lead a new ritual, be comforted that our God
likes to laugh.

If you feel that your design or participation in a
ritual is what makes it work, forget it. Let the
Spirit do her work.

If you feel that designing and leading a meaningful
ritual is a natural skill, you are wrong. The only
path to a good ritual is practice, practice, practice.

The authors of this booklet are eager to hear about your small Christian community's experiences in designing and executing rituals.

Please address your comments, questions and anxieties to: Ritual, Buena Vista, P.O. Box 745475, Arvada, CO 80006-5475, bv@buenavista.org.

Shared Prayer

Facilitator invites group members to quiet themselves for prayer, then reads this prayer aloud:

> Loving God, we hold in prayer before you all the concerns of our hearts and our lives. As a community we now share our prayers of thankfulness and of petition.

At this time, members share intentions for the community and personal intentions.

Closing Prayer

Loving God, thank you for this community. We praise you for the gifts you have given each one of us for the expression of your Spirit in our lives. Help us to continue to grow closer to each other and closer to you so that we may bring about the reign of God in this world. Through our ritual, help us to see more clearly what work needs to be done and give us the strength and wisdom for this work. *Amen.*

Further Reading

Baranowski, Arthur with Kathleen M. O'Reilly and Carrie M. Piro. *Praying Alone and Together.* Cincinnati: St. Anthony Messenger Press, 2000.

Begolly, Michael J. *Leading the Assembly in Prayer: A Practical Guide for Lay and Ordained Ministers.* San Jose: Resource Publications, 1997.

Cleary, William. *Psalm Services for Group Prayer.* Mystic, CT: Twenty-Third Publications, 1993.

Ditewig, William T. *Lay Leaders: Resources for the Changing Parish.* Notre Dame, IN: Ave Maria Press, 1991. (See especially chapter 5: The Lay Leader and Public Prayer.)

Hayes, Edward. *Prayers for the Domestic Church.* Leavenworth, KS: Forest of Peace Publishing, 1994.

Lee, Bernard, J., S.M. with William V. D'Antonio. *The Catholic Experience of Small Christian Communities.* New York/ Mahwah, NJ: Paulist Press, 2000.

Pile, Cindy, ed. *Our Prayers Rise Like Incense: Liturgies for Peace* Erie, PA: Pax Christi USA, 1998.

Rathschmidt, Jack, OFM CAP and Gaynell Bordes Cronin. *Rituals for Home and Parish.* Mahwah, N.J.: Paulist Press, 1996.

Trembley, Lo-Ann and David. *Pray with All Your Senses: Discovering the Wholeness Jesus Brings.* Chicago: ACTA Publications, 1999.

Wagner, Nick. *The 101 Most-Asked Questions about Liturgy.* San Jose: Resource Publications, 1996.

About the Authors

Fr. James Telthorst is a priest of the Archdiocese of St. Louis, ordained in 1968. After serving as an associate pastor, he obtained his Master's in Liturgical Studies from Notre Dame University and served as Director of the Office of Worship in St. Louis. He has served as pastor of the St. Louis Cathedral and is currently pastor of Our Lady of Sorrows parish.

Richard White, a longtime, active member of Buena Vista, is currently Director of Social Justice and Outreach for St. Patrick's Catholic Community, having served as Director of Christian Formation there as well. He is Co-chair of East Valley Interfaith, and President of Arizona Interfaith Network, dedicated to the development of leaders to address issues of local concern. Dick served as one of Buena Vista's representatives to the Joint Task Force for Small Christian Communities for several years. He earned his B.A. from St. Mary's College, his Master's in Divinity from DeAndreis Institute of Theology, and studied at Catholic University and DePaul University.

Felicia Wolf, O.S.F., a member of Buena Vista, is on faculty at the Institute of Pastoral Studies at Loyola University, Chicago. She is also Director of Religious Education in a multicultural, inner city parish. Having been a member of a religious community for over 40 years she is passionate about understanding the meaning and workings of communities. Currently, Felicia is working on her Ph.D. in Adult Theological Education. She also has a Master's from the University of Chicago in Education and a Master's from Loyola University in Pastoral Studies.